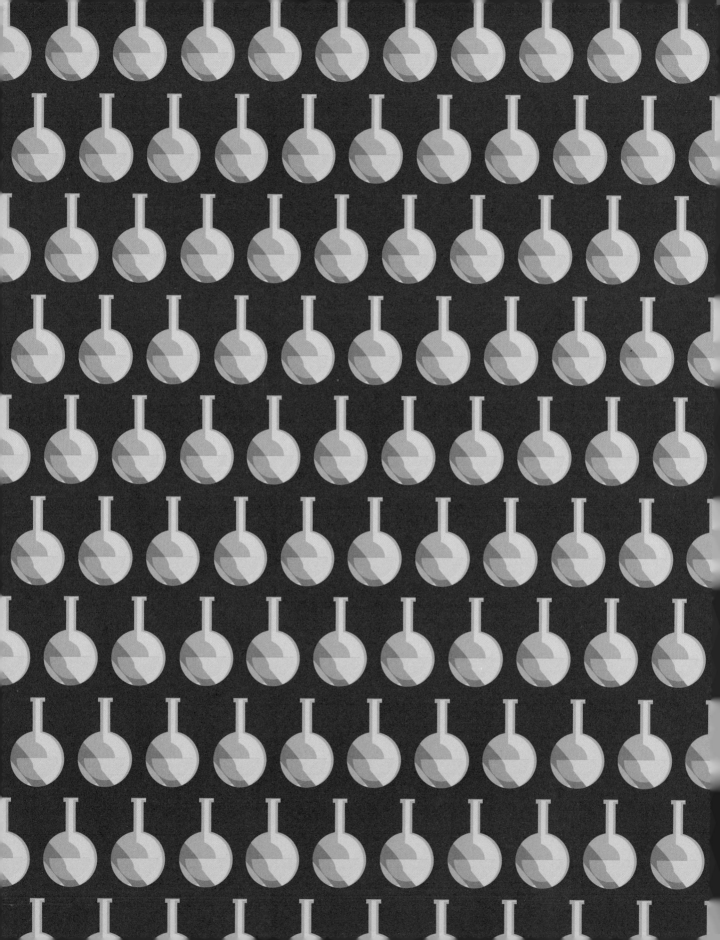

MARIE CURIE

GREAT LIVES IN GRAPHICS

Button
Books

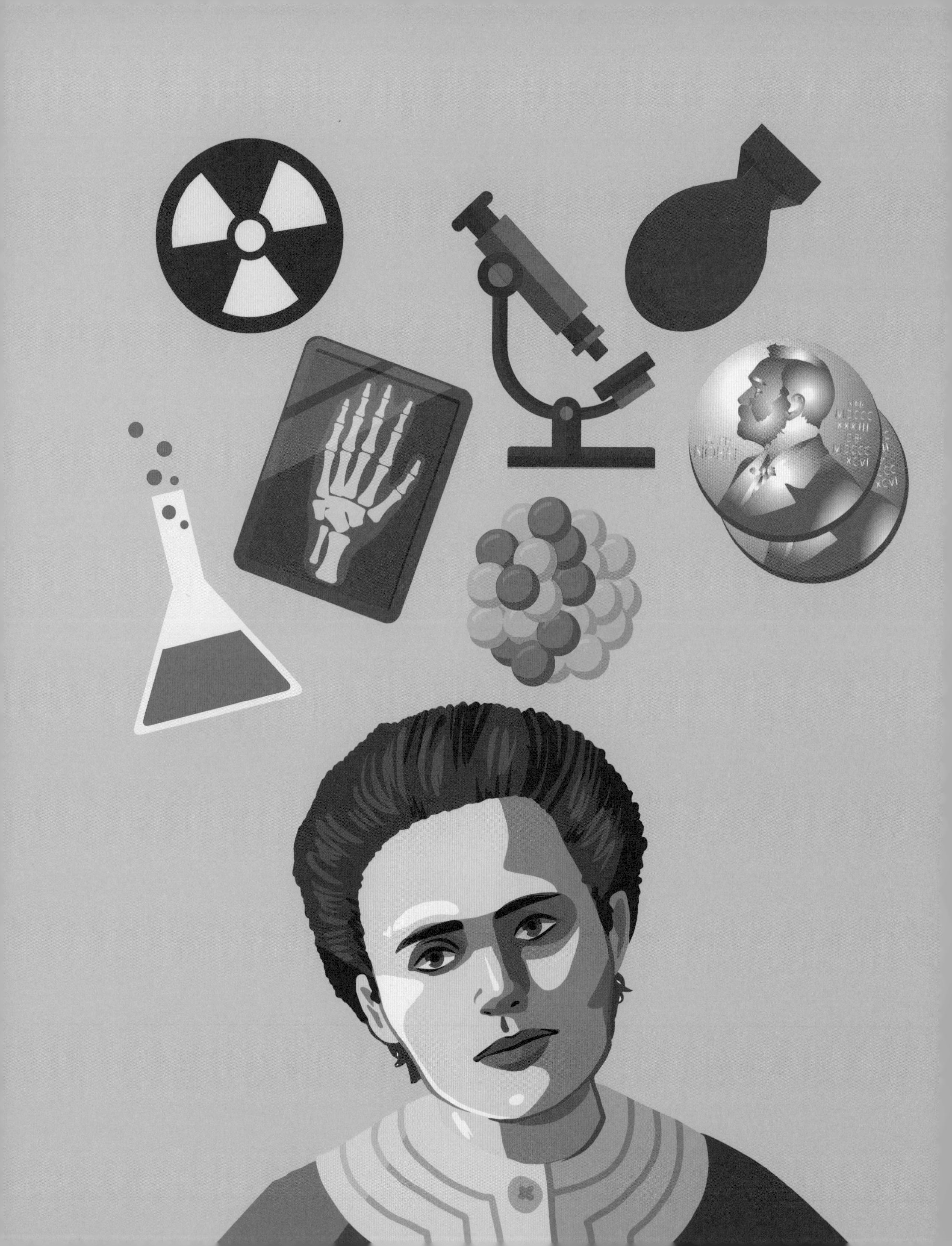

NOBEL
MDCCC
XXXIII
MDCCC
XCVI

Marie Curie was a scientific genius whose discoveries would transform the world in the 20th century. Thanks to her groundbreaking – and very dangerous! – investigations into the mysterious world of radioactivity, generations of scientists and inventors have been able to develop everything from treatments for cancer and nuclear power stations to the microwave oven! And what's even more impressive is that she did it at a time when women were mostly excluded from careers in science.

She became world-famous and won two Nobel Prizes, but Marie Curie never let her celebrity status go to her head. She remained quietly dedicated to scientific research and trying to make the world a better place. During World War One, she risked her life to treat soldiers at the frontline, using the X-ray research she had helped to pioneer. And after the war, when she wasn't working hard, she travelled to spread the word about the importance of scientific research. Her life had its fair share of tragedies, including prejudice, illness and sudden death, but her fighting spirit is part of what makes her so fascinating and inspiring. Let's meet this scientific icon…

MARIE'S WORLD

1896
The first modern Olympic Games take place in Paris

1897
Dracula by Bram Stoker published

1867
Marie Curie is born on 7 November in the Kingdom of Poland, which is then part of the Russian Empire

1896
Henri Becquerel discovers radioactivity

1898
Marie discovers the elements polonium and radium

84 **Po**

88 **Ra**

1869
Russian scientist Dmitri Mendeleev creates Periodic Table

1895
Marie marries fellow scientist, Pierre Curie, and they work together

1901
Queen Victoria dies

R.I.P. Queen Vicky

1879
American inventor Thomas Edison patents first light bulb

1891
Marie travels to Paris to study physics and chemistry

1903
Marie wins the Nobel Prize for physics

1886
The Statue of Liberty in New York is opened

1889
Eiffel Tower opens in Paris

1906
Pierre Curie dies. Marie becomes the first woman to teach at the Sorbonne

1911
Marie wins the Nobel Prize for chemistry

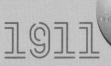

1934
Marie dies on 4 July aged 66 from a bone marrow disease caused by the effects of radiation

R.I.P. Marie

1935
Marie's daughter Irène wins the Nobel Prize for chemistry

1912
The Titanic sinks

1932
John Cockcroft and Ernest Walton split the atom for the first time

1936
The BBC launches the world's first regular hi-def TV service

1929
The Great Depression starts and causes misery worldwide

1937
The Hindenburg disaster takes place

1928
Alexander Fleming discovers penicillin, the first antibiotic

1945
The first nuclear bomb is detonated in New Mexico, USA

1914
WWI begins. Marie works at the frontline giving X-rays to wounded soldiers

1951
The first nuclear power plant produces usable electricity

1921
Marie visits the United States

1915
Albert Einstein publishes General Theory of Relativity

1917
The Russian Revolution marks the end of the Russian Empire

1995
Marie becomes the first woman to have her ashes housed in the Panthéon in Paris, a building dedicated to the memory of great French citizens

Baby BRAINIAC!

RUSSIAN EMPIRE

In the mid-19th and early 20th centuries, **Poland** was part of the **Russian Empire**, which stretched across large parts of Europe and Asia. It was ruled by the Russian tsars – or emperors – from 1721 until unrest and revolution forced the final tsar, **Nicholas II**, to give up the throne in 1917.

The Tsarist regime that controlled Poland during Marie's childhood tried to crush the independent Polish culture, making life difficult for ordinary Polish people like her family. The Russian authorities clamped down on the use of the Polish language, believing that it would be easier to absorb the country into the empire if its people had to speak the same language as their rulers.

NICHOLAS II

WARSAW

POLAND

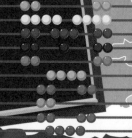

Both Marie's parents, Wladyslaw and Bronislawa, were teachers. Her father taught math and physics – Marie inherited his scientific skills.

Maria Salomea Skłodowska – later to become world-famous as **Marie Curie** – was born in the city of **Warsaw** in the Congress Kingdom of Poland. From a young age, it was obvious that she had exceptional gifts. But poverty, hardship and heartache meant that she would have to struggle to show the world her genius.

A star pupil, Marie **graduated** top of her class from secondary school, winning a gold medal. What would she do next?

RUSSIA

MEMORY GAME

Marie had an incredible memory from an early age.
How good is your memory? Look at the group of objects in the picture below for 30 seconds, then look away and see how many you can remember. Did you get them all right?

FAMILY TRAGEDY

The Curie family lived an ever more **precarious** life. Marie's parents struggled to find steady work because of the official bias against teaching in the Polish language. They were forced to move to smaller and smaller apartments because money was so tight. Sadly, Marie's mother died of **tuberculosis** when she was only 10. Her oldest sister also died of **typhus**. These experiences would affect Marie for the rest of her life.

TYPHUS
A disease spread by lice, fleas and mites. The symptoms include diarrhoea, a very high temperature and a dark spotty rash on the chest.

TUBERCULOSIS
A disease that mainly affects the lungs. The main symptom is a persistent cough that may bring up blood. Left untreated, it can eventually kill.

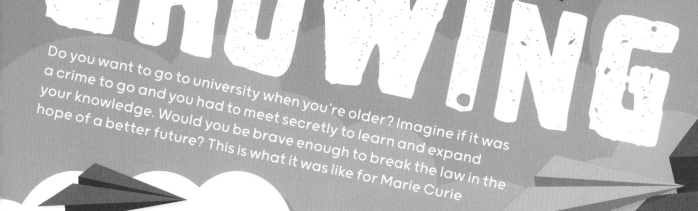

GROWING

Do you want to go to university when you're older? Imagine if it was a crime to go and you had to meet secretly to learn and expand your knowledge. Would you be brave enough to break the law in the hope of a better future? This is what it was like for Marie Curie

Women were not allowed to study in higher education in Poland during Marie Curie's youth. Only men could attend the university in Warsaw, while women were expected to stay at home, serving as wives and mothers. Marie had no legal route to continue her studies in her home country, despite being one of the brightest students.

FLYING UNI

TOP SECRET

A secret organisation, known as the 'flying university', gave Marie and her sister Bronya the opportunity to study in secret. The institution, active between 1883 and 1905, let Polish men and women study in their native language. They were taught by some of the best professors in Poland, who had been left unemployed when the Russian government shut down Polish universities. Small tuition fees were charged to pay for the teachers and books. By studying here, Marie and Bronya prepared for their future training abroad.

HOW DID THE FLYING UNIVERSITY ESCAPE DETECTION?

They used the following tricks:
* Students would meet in different locations throughout Warsaw, rather than using a fixed address.
* They would enter the location alone or in pairs, to avoid attracting attention.

WINGS

SUFFERING FOR SCIENCE!

Marie rented a tiny attic room to live nearer to the university. It was so cold at night that she had to wear all of her clothes to keep from freezing!

Bronya was the first to leave Poland, heading to the Sorbonne - a world-famous university in Paris - to train as a doctor. Marie was forced to remain behind in Poland and get a job to earn money to support her family, including her sister studying abroad.

In 1891, Bronya was able to let Marie stay with her in Paris. Marie jumped at the chance to leave Poland and study science at the Sorbonne. She went to lectures by famous physicists of the time and worked late into the night, quickly becoming one of the top students at the university, gaining two good degrees in physics and maths between 1893-1894.

THIS WAS A DANGEROUS JOB...

If she was caught, Marie might've been sent to prison or exiled to Siberia, a vast, remote and very cold northern region of Russia. But Marie was determined to do what she thought was right and in the best interests of her community – an attitude that she would carry with her throughout her life.

Marie became a governess: a woman who works as a private tutor for the children of wealthy parents. From 1886, she worked for a rich family in this role, but she continued to resist the Russian Empire. She would teach her students – and the children of local factory workers and peasants – so that they could read and write in Polish, helping to keep the language alive.

BREAD, BUTTER AND TEA

What Marie survived on during her time as a student.

X-TRAORDINARY!

Soon after Marie graduated, a physicist called Wilhelm Röntgen was experimenting with electricity when he noticed a mysterious glow in his lab. He realised it could be used to capture images of the inside of objects, and his accidental discovery kicked off a radiation revolution!

Inside Story

1 Before Marie was born, scientists such as **Michael Faraday and James Clerk Maxwell** had been busy investigating light and electricity and magnetism, and their experiments had begun to show that there was a connection between them.

2 On November 8, 1895, German physicist **Wilhelm Conrad Röntgen** was conducting an experiment in his lab, looking at what happened when he passed an electrical current through a special tube, when he noticed that a fluorescent screen nearby had **begun to glow**.

3 This wouldn't have been so **surprising** if there was nothing between the screen and the tube, but for this experiment Röntgen had surrounded the tube with thick cardboard!

4 The tube seemed to be producing **invisible rays** that could pass through solid objects! What were these mysterious rays? He thought they might be similar to light, but then how did they pass through the cardboard? Röntgen didn't know, so he **called them 'X' rays**.

5 Röntgen tried putting different objects between the tube and the screen, but **the screen still glowed**. Then he put his hand in front of the tube and a **shadowy image** of the bones inside it was projected onto the screen!

6 Not only had Röntgen accidentally discovered a new type of **invisible radiation**, he'd also stumbled across its most important use!

What are X-rays?

X-rays are essentially super powerful rays of light. Both are types of **electromagnetic radiation.**

HOW electro magnetic radiation interacts with the body

Radiation is **energy that's moving**, and it's all around you. **Light**, **heat** and **X-rays** are examples, and they all travel in **waves**. Just like waves in the ocean, electromagnetic waves have **crests** and **troughs**. The distance from the top of one wave to the next is called a **wavelength**. The **shorter** the wavelength, the **more energy** the wave has. Because X-rays have a much higher energy than visible light, they can **pass through most objects**, including your body!

gamma rays

x-rays

ultraviolet

visible light

infra red

microwaves

radio waves

IN THE HOSPITAL

※ When an X-ray machine is turned on, X-rays travel through a patient's body and hit a special detector or film on the other side.

※ As they pass through, they're absorbed in different amounts by the different tissues.

※ Because more is absorbed by bones than muscle or fat, they show up as different shades on the film. Bones appear white, while other tissues look grey.

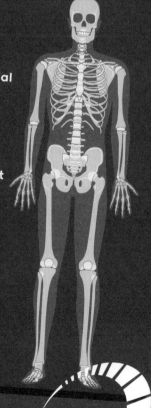

ALL ELECTROMAGNETIC RADIATION TRAVELS AT THE SPEED OF LIGHT IN A VACUUM, WHICH IS

300,000KM per second

RADIATION REVOLUTION

A few months after Röntgen stumbled on X-rays, French physicist Antoine Henri Becquerel made another incredible accidental discovery

1

After hearing about Röntgen's work, **Becquerel** began looking for a connection between **phosphoresence** (when a substance slowly gives off light after it absorbs energy) and the mysterious **new X-rays.**

THAT'S A FACT!

GLOW-IN-THE-DARK STICKERS ARE PHOSPHORESCENT

THAT'S BANANAS!

Bananas are radioactive! Every banana contains high levels of the chemical element potassium, which is slightly radioactive. Don't worry though, it's such a tiny amount of radioactivity that it isn't at all dangerous. Phew!

YOU'D HAVE TO EAT 10 MILLION IN ONE GO TO DIE OF RADIATION POISONING!

3

Becquerel realised that the uranium was giving off **radiation** all the time, on its own! **He'd discovered radioactivity!**

2

Becquerel found that some minerals, such as **uranium**, glowed (or phosphoresced) when placed in the sun. On a cloudy day in 1896, he stored his uranium in a drawer alongside some photographic plates, and was amazed to find on his return that the uranium had **marked the plate** even without sunlight.

HENRI BECQUEREL

WHAT IS RADIOACTIVITY?

Everything you see around you is made up of elements, and these are built of atoms. Most of these atoms are STABLE. That means the nucleus in the middle of the atom has a good balance of neutrons and protons.

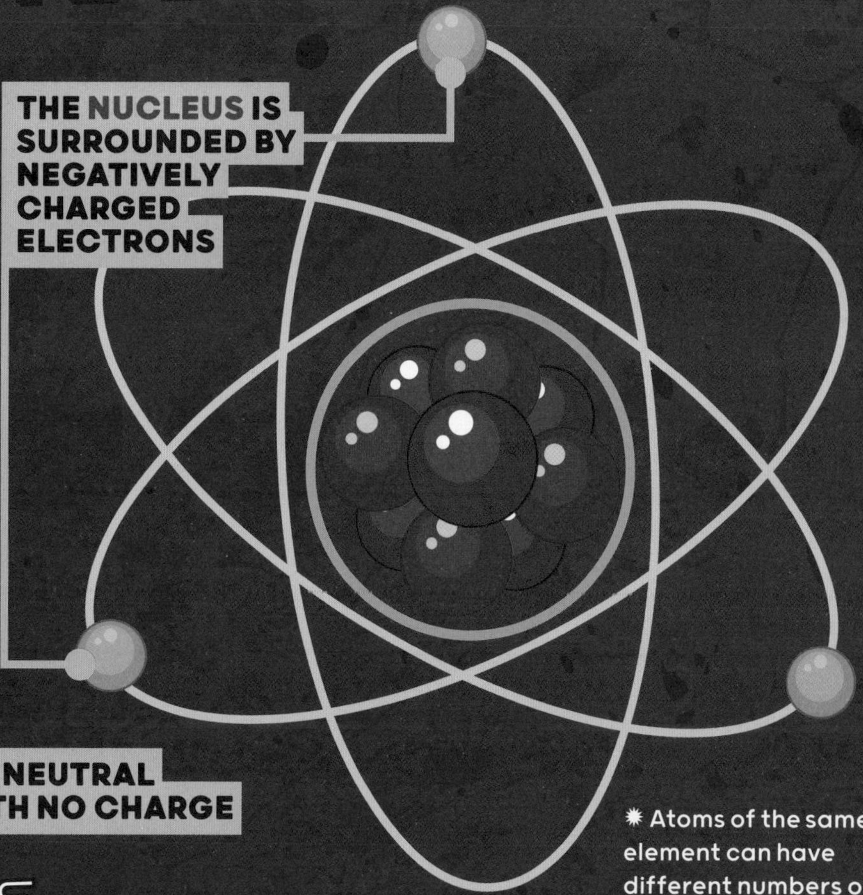

THE NUCLEUS IS SURROUNDED BY NEGATIVELY CHARGED ELECTRONS

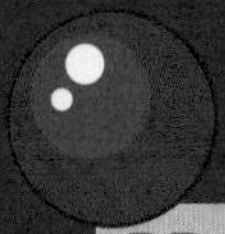

PROTONS ARE PARTICLES WITH A POSITIVE CHARGE

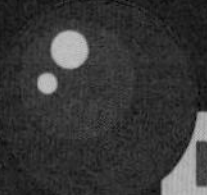

NEUTRONS ARE NEUTRAL PARTICLES, WITH NO CHARGE

✷ Atoms of the same element can have different numbers of neutrons in the nucleus.

✷ If there are too many or too few neutrons, then an atom can become **UNSTABLE**.

✷ That means it starts to feel uncomfortable, a bit like you might do when you're about to sneeze, but it hasn't come out yet!

✷ To feel more balanced, the atom shoots out particles or rays of energy. When this happens, **WE CALL IT RADIOACTIVITY**.

STABLE ATOMS

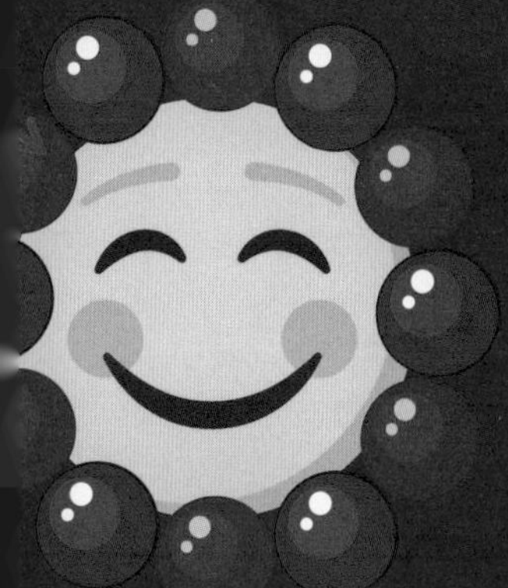

CARBON 12
6 PROTONS
6 NEUTRONS

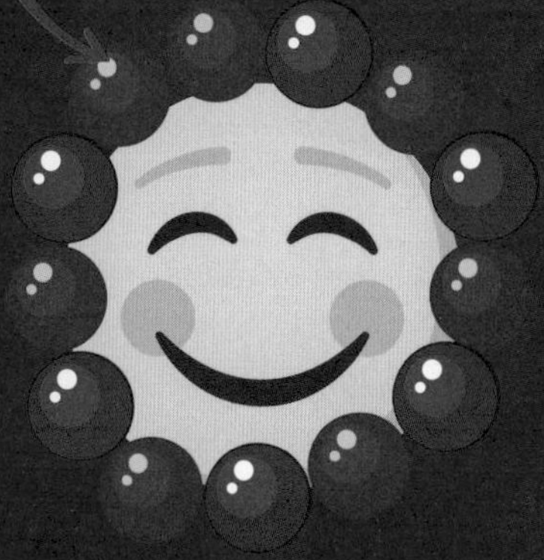

CARBON 13
6 PROTONS
7 NEUTRONS

UNSTABLE ATOM

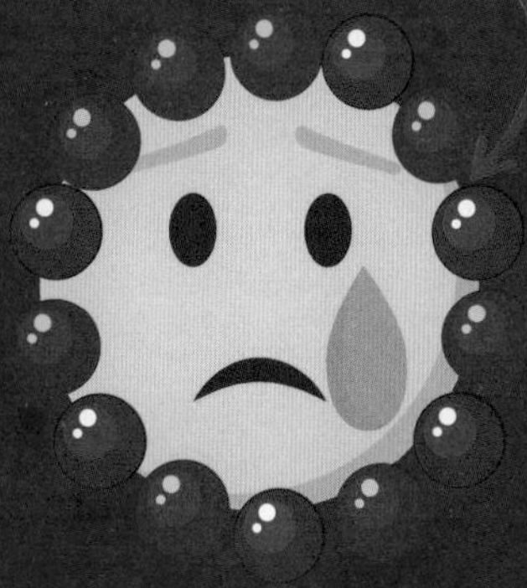

CARBON 14
6 PROTONS
8 NEUTRONS

DIRTY WORK

1
ELEMENT OF SURPRISE

Marie wanted to build on Henri Becquerel's research into radioactivity, so she carried out her own. She experimented with different uranium compounds and made an important discovery: the more uranium they contained, the more radiation they gave off. This showed that an element's ability to radiate didn't depend on the arrangement of their atoms in a compound, but on something in the atoms themselves.

2
BANG GOES THE THEORY

The idea that the radioactive rays might be caused by the structure of the atom itself would prove to be revolutionary. Until this point, most scientists had thought that the atom was the most elementary particle and that it couldn't be divided into any other smaller parts. Marie's discoveries suggested this theory was false.

3
PECULIAR PITCHBLENDE

Marie quickly focused her attention on pitchblende: a mineral made of different elements, mostly of uranium. The radioactivity of pitchblende proved to be greater than that of pure uranium, which could only be explained if there were small elements of an even more radioactive but unknown substance within it...

4
SEIZING SAMPLES

Marie got hold of samples of pitchblende from geological museums and studied it with her husband in his laboratory. In 1898, they were able to extract two new highly radioactive elements from the pitchblende: polonium and radium. They named polonium after Poland, Marie's home country. They started to use the word radioactivity to refer to this radiation for the first time.

Marie met the well-known French physical chemist Pierre Curie in 1894 and they soon fell in love. They had similar personalities, both valuing hard work and the pursuit of scientific knowledge over fame or fortune. They were married the following year and began a scientific partnership that would lead to world-changing discoveries

POLONIUM IS 300x

MORE RADIOACTIVE THAN URANIUM!

7 TOP MARKS

In 1903, Marie Curie presented her findings in her doctoral thesis. The members of her examination committee declared it to be a great contribution to science.

5 BREAK TIME

In order to prove that polonium and radium really were new elements, Marie and Pierre needed to produce them in greater amounts. They obtained tonnes of pitchblende from the slag-heaps at a mine in Bohemia and had it transported to their new facilities in a large unused shed. Here they would spend days separating the chemical elements from the waste material. It was exhausting work: Marie had to sift out any debris from the piles of pitchblende and then physically break it down.

HOME SWEET HOME

Doing super important scientific work in a draughty old shed wasn't easy. It was…

 HOT IN THE SUMMER

 FREEZING IN THE WINTER

 COVERED WITH A LEAKY GLASS ROOF

6 GLOW IN THE DARK

At night, the radioactive elements Marie and Pierre extracted would give off a luminous glow. It was pretty to look at, but dangerous.

8 PRIZEWINNERS

The same year, Marie and Pierre shared the Nobel Prize in Physics with Henri Becquerel for their pioneering work on radiation. Marie became the first woman to win a Nobel Prize. The award made them famous and brought this strange new science to public attention.

FIRST WOMAN TO WIN NOBEL PRIZE

SOMETIMES I HAD TO SPEND A WHOLE DAY STIRRING A BOILING MASS WITH A HEAVY IRON ROD NEARLY AS BIG AS MYSELF. I WOULD BE BROKEN WITH FATIGUE AT DAY'S END

1901

First year the Nobel Prize is awarded

THE MERCHANT OF DEATH!

How Nobel was described by one newspaper article. Maybe he thought the prizes would change his reputation?

EYES ON

WHO WAS ALFRED NOBEL? (1833-1896)

A child prodigy with an intense interest in explosives, Alfred Nobel invented dynamite and built a network of factories to manufacture it for sale. This new explosive material was key to the evolution of the modern industrialised world. It was used to blast tunnels and build railways, roads and canals. The success of dynamite and the other explosives Nobel created made him a very wealthy man.

After his death, it was revealed that Nobel had left most of his fortune for the establishment of the Nobel Prizes. We don't know exactly why, but it's been suggested that he wanted to ensure the world would remember him for something inspiring and positive rather than for producing highly explosive materials that had come to be used as deadly weapons.

FAMOUS WINNERS

ALBERT EINSTEIN
General Theory of Relativity

MARTIN LUTHER KING, JR
Leader of the civil rights movement in the US

NIELS BOHR
Modelled the atom

61

Nobel Prizes have been awarded to women

THE PRIZE

Winning a Nobel Prize is widely considered to be one of the greatest honours in the world. Set up by the Swedish inventor and businessman Alfred Nobel in his will, the six prizes are meant to reward people or teams who have done groundbreaking and world-changing work in…

PHYSICS CHEMISTRY
MEDICINE ECONOMICS
PEACE-MAKING LITERATURE

989 people and organisations have won

Marie Curie is the only woman to win **2** NOBEL PRIZES

WILHELM RÖNTGEN
Discoverer of X-rays. He won the first-ever Nobel Prize for physics!

IRÈNE JOLIOT-CURIE
Marie's daughter, who continued her work on radioactivity

ALEXANDER FLEMING
Developed the first antibiotics

HERMANN J MULLER
Proved the dangers of radiation

JAMES WATSON, FRANCIS CRICK AND MAURICE WILKINS
Discovered the structure of DNA

NELSON MANDELA
Worked to end apartheid in South Africa

SOME FAMOUS SCIENTISTS WHO NEVER WON

DMITRI MENDELEEV
Creator of the Periodic Table

THOMAS EDISON
Inventor of the lightbulb

GEORGES LEMAITRE
Big Bang theory

EDWIN HUBBLE
Proved that the universe is expanding

STEPHEN HAWKING
Developed theory of black holes

NIKOLA TESLA
Developed the AC electric system

MARIE v THE PRESS

Despite her great achievements, Marie Curie found the French press turning on her from 1910 onwards. Why did they want to make her into a villain in the eyes of the public?

REJECTED!

The antisemitic newspaper <u>L'Action Française</u> started a campaign to stop Marie Curie from being elected into the French Academy of Sciences, a prestigious organisation of important scientists. The newspaper appealed to widespread prejudice against foreigners, women and Jewish people to argue why Marie Curie should not be voted into the academy (Curie was Polish and a woman but not Jewish, although the newspaper implied that she was). The campaign succeeded and Marie was denied entry, a decision that she found very hurtful.

XENOPHOBIA: FEAR/HATRED OF PEOPLE FROM ANOTHER COUNTRY

INSULTED!

MARIE GO HOME

In 1911, the press began a new smear campaign, claiming that Marie was having an affair with a married colleague, Paul Langevin. Instead of giving coverage to the fact that she'd won a second Nobel Prize, the press encouraged the public to hound Marie out of France. On one occasion, an angry crowd gathered outside her house, throwing stones and calling for her to go back to Poland.

ANTISEMITISM
Hatred and prejudice against Jewish people

MISOGYNY
Hatred of women

DUEL AT DAWN!

The furious Paul Langevin challenged the editor of one newspaper to a duel with pistols. Luckily, no shots were fired and no one was killed!

Marie tried her best to carry on with her life during these campaigns against her, travelling to Stockholm in December to give her Nobel lecture. However, the stress eventually became too much and she was taken to hospital to recover from a period of depression.

IN FRANCE IN 1910, women were badly treated and had few rights. They couldn't vote or demand equal pay

1944: the year women finally gained the right to vote in France

HEALTH HAZARDS

Back in Marie's time, the harmful side effects of radioactive materials weren't well understood. Marie and Pierre spent all day every day living and working among these dangerous elements and started to show signs of serious sickness

BURNS & CRACKED SKIN

SWEET DREAMS?

Marie kept a mound of glowing radium salts on her bedside table as a night light!

FRAIL

LETHAL LEGACY

Marie's daughter Irène and son-in-law Frédéric continued her work – both died of diseases induced by radiation.

X-CELLENT!

In the right amounts, radiation can be used for good. X-rays help doctors make diagnoses. Doctors also use powerful X-ray beams to zap cancerous cells and kill them.

NEARLY BLIND
from cataracts

ALWAYS TIRED

FEELING SICK

DEATH AGED 66

from anaemia caused by radiation exposure

1000+ yrs

How long some of Marie's notebooks will stay radioactive! Today, tourists have to sign a waiver to read them.

TRAGEDY!

On 19 April, 1906, Pierre was struck by a horse-drawn wagon in Paris and killed instantly. Marie was devastated, but kept working for the sake of her daughters.

POOR PIERRE

SCARRED HANDS   SHAKY LEGS   CONSTANT PAIN

✳ Pierre carried a sample of radium in his pocket to show colleagues how it gave off heat and shone in the dark.

✳ He experimented on himself, wrapping a band of radium salts around his arm and studying the burn-like wound that developed and left a grey scar!

X-RAY VISION

When World War One began in 1914, Marie Curie created mobile X-ray units called 'Little Curies' to treat wounded soldiers on the battlefield

21C151

WHEN THE WAR BROKE OUT...

Marie **travelled from Paris to Bordeaux** carrying her supply of radium in a 20kg lead container, which she left there in a bank vault for safekeeping.

FOR THE REST OF THE WAR...

Marie and her daughter Irène dedicated themselves to developing the science of **X-radiography**: using radiation to produce images of the insides of the body that could be used to diagnose and treat patients.

I AM **RESOLVED** TO PUT ALL MY STRENGTH AT THE SERVICE OF MY **ADOPTED** COUNTRY, SINCE I CANNOT DO ANYTHING FOR MY **UNFORTUNATE** NATIVE COUNTRY JUST NOW...

THE TWO SIDES IN THE WAR

THE ALLIED POWERS
GREAT BRITAIN
FRANCE
RUSSIA
ITALY
ROMANIA
CANADA
JAPAN
UNITED STATES

THE CENTRAL POWERS
GERMANY
AUSTRIA-HUNGARY
BULGARIA
OTTOMAN EMPIRE

16M+ PEOPLE
DIED IN WWI

THE RED CROSS
AN INDEPENDENT ORGANISATION THAT PROVIDES AID TO PEOPLE AROUND THE WORLD IN EMERGENCY SITUATIONS LIKE WARS AND NATURAL DISASTERS.

MARIE CONVINCED THE FRENCH GOVERNMENT...
to set up the country's first **military radiology centres**. She was appointed director of the **Red Cross** Radiology Service there. She had vans – called radiology cars – and field hospitals equipped with simple X-ray technology that could be used to examine injured soldiers at the battle front.

MARIE TAUGHT HERSELF...
to **drive a car** and learned basic human anatomy so that she'd be able to personally take part in the project. She trained **150 young women** in how to use the X-ray machinery so that they could also drive the vans and help the soldiers. Marie and Irène drove two of the vans themselves.

20
RADIOLOGY CARS

LITTLE CURIES
WHAT SOLDIERS NAMED THE RADIOLOGY CARS

MARIE OFFERED TO...
have her two golden Nobel Prize medals **melted down** to pay for the radiology service, but she was refused. Instead, she convinced wealthy friends to give money to buy equipment and vehicles.

In the 1910s, word spread about Marie Curie's experiments and discovery of radium. Before long, the element had sparked people's imaginations and entrepreneurs were ready to make money from it – with some horrible consequences

THE GREAT RADIUM CRAZE!

A MIRACLE CURE?

Radium was used to treat some forms of cancer by destroying cancerous cells, but this led to a popular – and mistaken – belief that it could be used to cure all kinds of ailments, or even prevent ageing!

COMPANIES STARTED TO MARKET RADIUM:

- ALARM CLOCKS
- WATER FOUNTAINS
- MAKE-UP
- WATER
- TOOTHPASTE

The public was fascinated by radium because it glowed in the dark!

RADIUM O'CLOCK

An American company called the US Radium Corporation set up factories to manufacture radium-paint-coated watch dials and airplane instrument panels, with its customers including the American military during World War One.

THE RADIUM GIRLS

The many young women who worked in these factories were given no safety precautions. They worked with radium all day long, even licking the brushes they used to paint to keep the tips pointed. At the end of the day, they would go home glowing because of the radium paint on their clothes and skin!

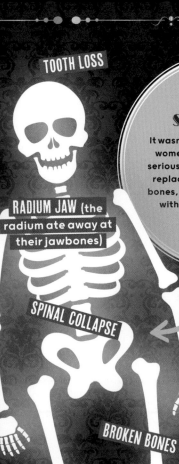

TOOTH LOSS

RADIUM JAW (the radium ate away at their jawbones)

SPINAL COLLAPSE

BROKEN BONES

SERIOUS SYMPTOMS

It wasn't long before these poor women started to experience serious health problems. Radium replaces the calcium in human bones, irradiating a person from within. The factory workers started to suffer:

SAFETY FIRST

The tragic case of the Radium Girls led to major changes:

Safety protocols were put in place to protect people working with radioactive materials, such as during the Manhattan Project (the project to build the world's first atomic bomb) ✓

The law was changed in the US in 1949 so that workers could seek compensation for illnesses caused by working ✓

TRACES OF THE PAST

Although the companies making radium-coated products in Paris went out of business decades ago, tiny amounts of radium can still be found on the floors and back gardens of buildings in the city. But these traces are too small to pose serious health risks.

50+

RADIUM FACTORY WORKERS WERE DEAD BY 1927

American adventure

When Marie Curie was interviewed by a prominent American journalist, Marie Maloney – known as Missy – a plan was hatched by the writer to help the scientist secure more radium for her laboratory, which only had just over 1 gram of the substance. By comparison, there were around 50 grams at the use of scientists in the US

Missy launched a press campaign to get the public behind Marie's request and convinced the very shy genius to do a public tour of the US and accept a gram of radium in person from the President!

'THE MARIE CURIE RADIUM FUND'

This is what Missy named her campaign. It sought to raise $100,000 dollars through public donations – the market value of a gram of radium. It was aimed at ordinary American women and the money was raised in one year.

1 SPRING, 1921

Marie Curie arrives in New York. A reception is held for her at the famous Carnegie Hall. Three thousand, five hundred members of the International Federation of University Women are there.

This is followed by a party at the swanky Waldorf Astoria hotel, where she is greeted by 500 representatives of different scientific organisations.

2 SMITH COLLEGE, MASSACHUSETTS

Two thousand college students sing a choral tribute to Curie before awarding her an honorary degree.

3 20 MAY, 1921, THE WHITE HOUSE, WASHINGTON DC

Marie Curie is presented with a parchment scroll and a key to a casket containing the gram of radium by President Warren Harding. The radium is fake – the real stuff is kept in the factory because it would be too dangerous to show in public.

1929

Marie makes a second trip to the US and receives another gram of radium, which she donates to the Radium Institute in Warsaw, Poland.

The end... and the beginning

Sadly, Marie Curie would die of leukaemia caused by her dangerous work with radioactive substances on 4 July, 1934, aged only 66. But her amazing achievements live on. Thanks to the pioneering work of Marie Curie, we really do live in a radioactive world!

GOING NUCLEAR

Marie Curie pioneered the science of radioactivity, but major new discoveries and innovations have continued to be made in the century since her work

THE GOOD...

RADIOCARBON DATING

Carbon-14 is a naturally radioactive isotope that forms in the upper atmosphere. All living things take in carbon during their lives, including small amounts of carbon-14. After death, a living thing stops taking in more carbon and so the level of carbon-14 begins to decline due to radioactive decay. By measuring the amount of carbon-14 in a dead organism, scientists can determine its approximate age. This is called radiocarbon dating.

MEDICINE

Slightly artificially radioactive substances can now be given to patients and used to diagnose illnesses or conditions in specific organs. X-rays and radioactive substances like iodine are also used to kill some types of cancer cells.

3.6BN X-RAYS ARE PERFORMED EVERY YEAR!

SCIENTIFIC RESEARCH

Researchers can slightly irradiate objects in order to track their movements and study things like the path that air or water pollution takes through an environment, or the direction of ocean currents.

MICROWAVE OVEN

In 1946, the microwave oven is invented by accident when an engineer called Perry Spencer is working on a radar magnetron – a device for producing electromagnetic waves used in early radar systems – and finds that it has melted the snack in his pocket. The microwave oven didn't catch on in a big way until 1967.

BREAKTHROUGH

In 1934, Irène Joliot-Curie and her husband Frédéric discovered artificial radioactivity: that a substance can be made radioactive by being bombarded with particles. This proved that radioactivity isn't limited to those elements that have natural radioactivity, like radium.

$2K COST OF THE FIRST MICROWAVE OVEN, THE 'RADARANGE', PRODUCED IN 1947

SPLITTING THE ATOM

In 1938, nuclear fission is discovered: when radioactive atoms like uranium are bombarded with neutron particles they split into simpler atoms, releasing enormous amounts of energy. This milestone would lead to the development of nuclear reactors for generating lots of electricity.

THE BAD...

NUCLEAR BOMBS

In the late 1930s and 1940s, scientists started to realise that the massive amounts of energy released in nuclear fission could be used to build a very powerful bomb.

THE BIG BANG

On 16 July, the first detonation of an atomic bomb takes place in New Mexico in the US. In August, two atomic bombs are dropped on Hiroshima and Nagasaki in Japan, killing 129,000-226,000 people and finally ending the Second World War.

1946

PHYSICAL CHEMIST WILLARD F LIBBY COMES UP WITH THE IDEA FOR RADIOCARBON DATING

INDUSTRY

Radiation can be used to:

Sterilise medical equipment

Kill pests that attack crops

Kill germs on food, helping it last longer

Remove polluting chemicals from the environment

IN NUCLEAR POWER PLANTS...

NUCLEAR FISSION IS USED TO HEAT WATER AND TURN IT INTO STEAM TO SPIN THE BLADES OF A TURBINE AND GENERATE ELECTRICITY

1951

EBR-I IN IDAHO, US, WAS THE FIRST NUCLEAR POWER PLANT TO PRODUCE ELECTRICITY THROUGH FISSION. IT IS NOW A MUSEUM

58 MEGATONS

THE YIELD OF THE LARGEST NUCLEAR BOMB EVER DETONATED. IT WAS EXPLODED BY THE USSR IN OCTOBER 1961

AND THE SILLY...

WATER GOOD IDEA!

First nuclear-powered submarine launched by the US Navy in 1954: the USS Nautilus.

X-ray machines were used in shoe shops to check that children's and adults' new shoes fitted properly. They were marketed as 'shoe-fitting fluoroscopes'. You could literally see the bones in your feet if you stuck them inside the contraption. When it became apparent that exposure to the waves could cause radiation burns or bone cancer, the machines were no longer used.

COMING IN

1ST WOMAN IN SPACE
The Russian astronaut (or cosmonaut) Valentina Tereshkova. On 16 June, 1963, she completed 48 orbits of the Earth in 71 hours.

1ST WOMAN TO FLY SOLO ACROSS THE ATLANTIC OCEAN
American aviator Amelia Earhart completed the solo flight in 1928 and became a celebrity. Sadly, she disappeared during another flight in 1937.

1ST WOMAN TO MAKE A SOLO ROUND-THE-WORLD FLIGHT
American pilot Jerrie Mock in 1964, setting off from Columbus, Ohio.

1ST FEMALE BLACK AMERICAN BILLIONAIRE
Businesswoman Sheila Johnson founded the cable TV channel Black Entertainment Network.

1ST DEMOCRATICALLY ELECTED FEMALE PRESIDENT
Icelandic politician Vigdís Finnbogadóttir was elected President of Iceland in 1980.

1ST FEMALE PRIME MINISTER OF THE UK
Margaret Thatcher served as Prime Minister from 1979 to 1990.

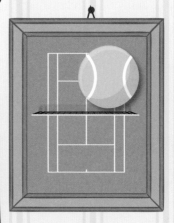

1ST PERSON TO ACHIEVE A CAREER GOLDEN SLAM IN SINGLES AND DOUBLES IN TENNIS
Serena Williams, widely considered one of the greatest tennis players of all time.

1ST WOMAN TO REACH THE SUMMIT OF MOUNT EVEREST
Japanese mountaineer Junko Tabei made it to the top on 16 May, 1975.

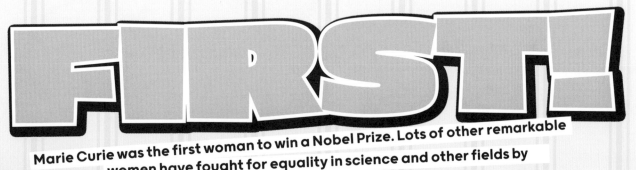

FIRST!

Marie Curie was the first woman to win a Nobel Prize. Lots of other remarkable women have fought for equality in science and other fields by accomplishing fantastic firsts. Here are just a few of them...

1ST COMPUTER PROGRAMMER
Mathematician Ada Lovelace wrote and published what is often considered the world's first machine algorithm for an early computing machine in 1843.

1ST PROFESSIONAL FEMALE HOT AIR BALLOONIST
French aeronaut Sophie Blanchard, who made her first solo ascent in 1805.

1ST WOMAN TO WIN AN OSCAR FOR BEST DIRECTOR
American filmmaker Kathryn Bigelow in 2010 for the war movie *The Hurt Locker*.

1ST QUEEN TO RULE ENGLAND
Mary I, also known as Bloody Mary, who reigned from 1553-1558.

1ST FEMALE PHARAOH OF ANCIENT EGYPT
Sobekneferu, who ruled from c1760-1756BC.

1ST WOMAN TO SWIM THE ENGLISH CHANNEL
American swimmer and Olympic champion Gertrude Caroline Ederle successfully crossed the Channel on her second attempt on 6 August, 1926, at the age of 19.

1ST FEMALE VICE-PRESIDENT OF THE US
Attorney Kamala Harris began serving in the post in 2021.

1ST WOMAN TO WIN THE NOBEL PEACE PRIZE
Baroness Bertha Felicie Sophie von Suttner (what a mouthful!) who won in 1905, partly for her popular anti-war novel called *Lay Down Your Arms*.

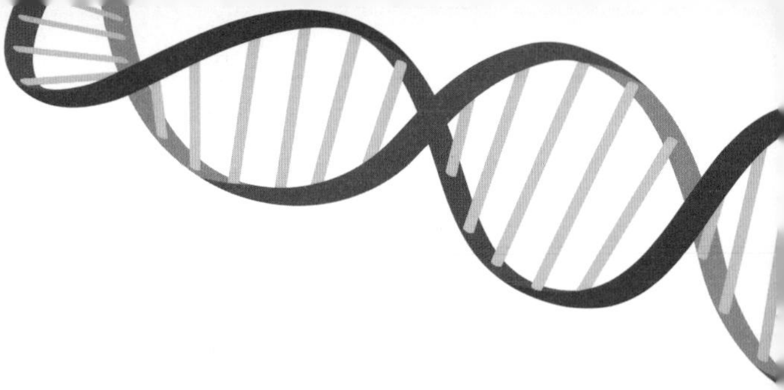

GLOSSARY

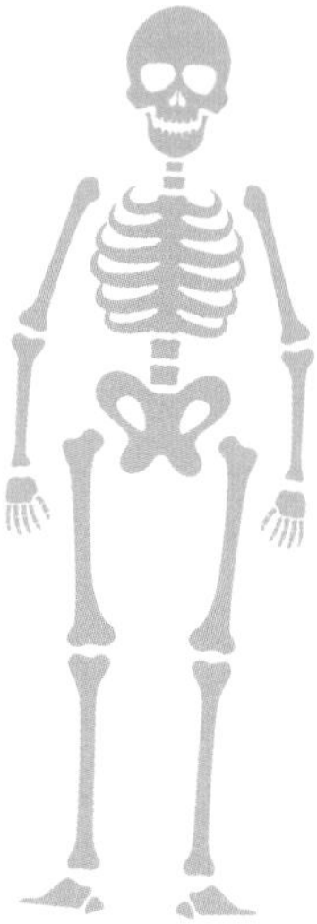

Ailment
An illness.

Anatomy
The bodily structure and inner workings of humans or animals.

Chemistry
The field of science concerned with the substances out of which matter is made and their reactions.

Debris
Scattered rubbish and rubble.

Dynamite
An explosive moulded into stick shapes and used to blow things up in war or in industries like construction.

Empire
A large group of countries and people that are ruled over by a single power.

Industrialised
When a country or a region contains modern businesses and factories producing goods.

Mineral
Solid substances that occur in the natural world.

Particles
The tiny pieces of matter inside an atom, such as electrons, neutrons and photons.

Physics
The field of science concerned with the nature of matter - including atoms - and energy, and how they behave.

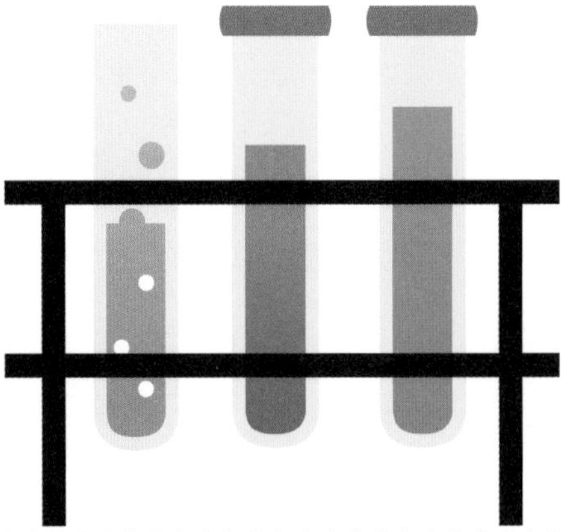

Pollution
When harmful substances and waste products are introduced into a natural environment and do damage to it.

Regime
A government that uses force to rule its citizens.

Sterilise
To clean an object of harmful bacteria and germs to make it safe for use.

Tsar
One of the all-powerful emperors who ruled Russia before the 1917 revolution.

USSR
A massive Communist empire centred in Russia that lasted from 1917 to 1991.

Vacuum
A space that contains no matter at all.

First published 2023 by Button Books, an imprint of Guild of Master Craftsman Publications Ltd, Castle Place, 166 High Street, Lewes, East Sussex, BN7 1XU, UK. Copyright in the Work © GMC Publications Ltd, 2023. ISBN 978 1 78708 133 8. Distributed by Publishers Group West in the United States. All rights reserved. No part of this publication may be reproduced, stored in a retrieval system, or transmitted in any form or by any means without the prior permission of the publisher and copyright owner. While every effort has been made to obtain permission from the copyright holders for all material used in this book, the publishers will be pleased to hear from anyone who has not been appropriately acknowledged and to make the correction in future reprints. The publishers and authors can accept no legal responsibility for any consequences arising from the application of information, advice, or instructions given in this publication. A catalogue record for this book is available from the British Library. Senior Project Editor: Nick Pierce. Design: Tim Lambert, Dean Chillmaid. Illustrations: Alex Bailey, Matt Carr, Shutterstock. Colour origination by GMC Reprographics. Printed and bound in China.

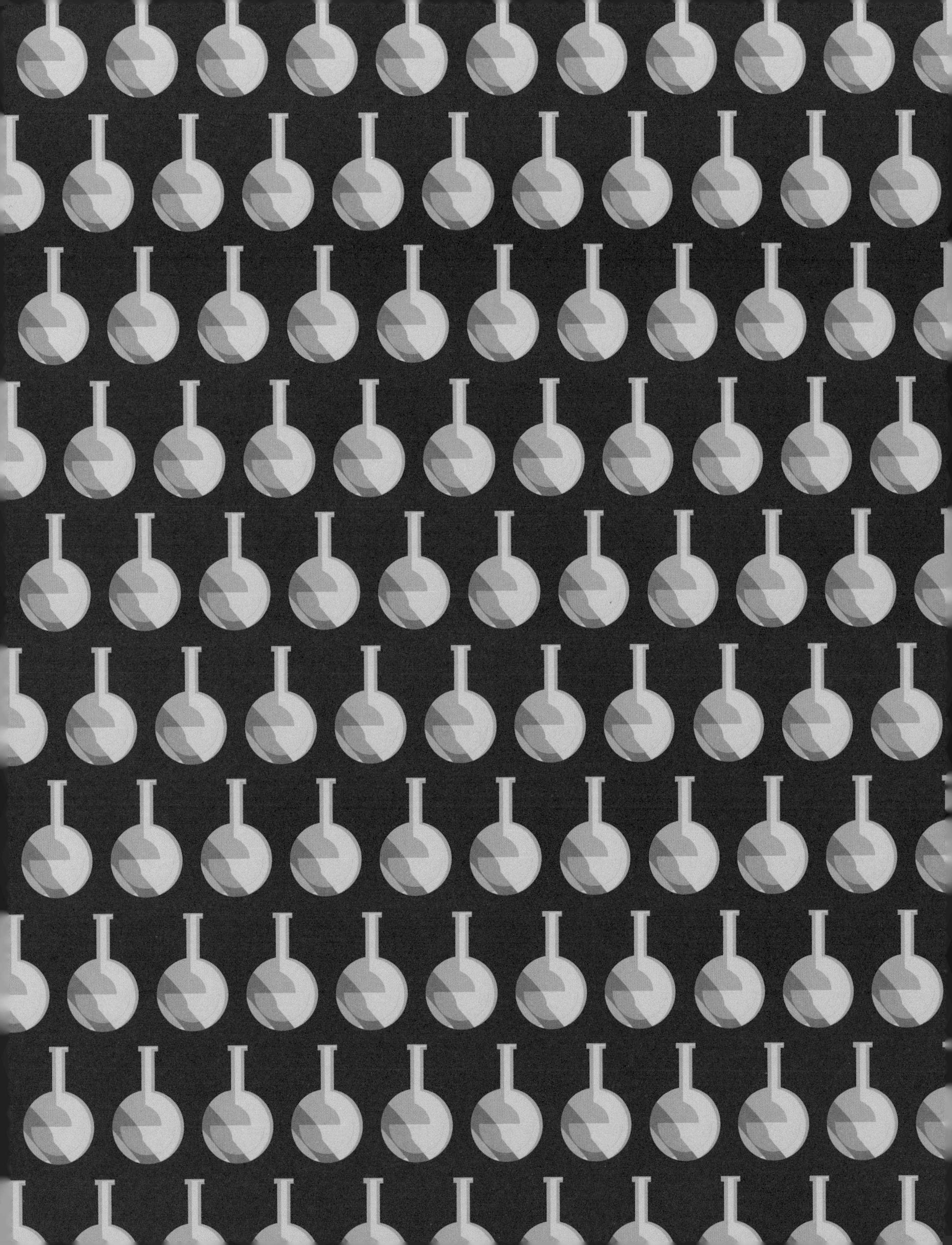

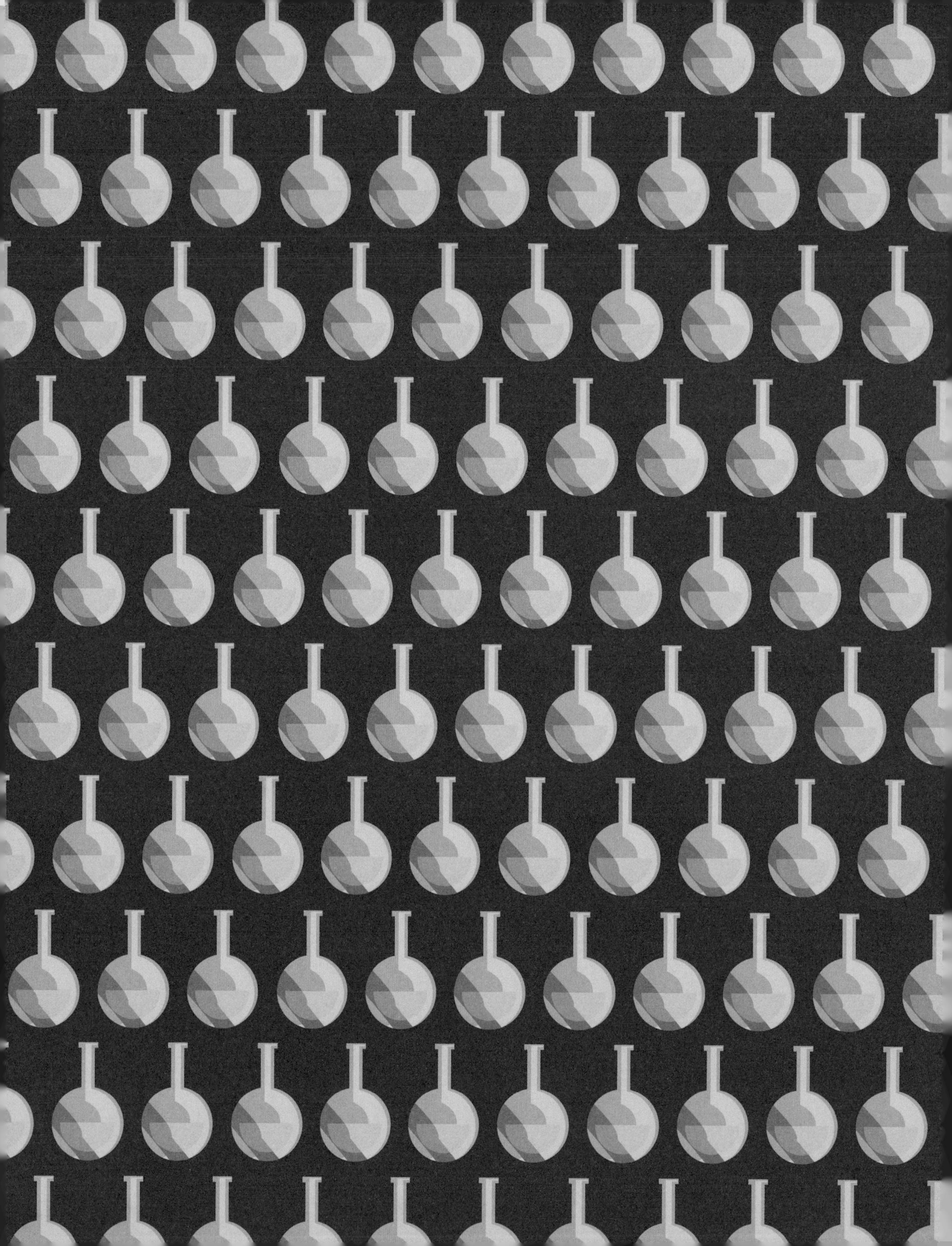